COPYRIGHT 2019 BY PATRICK HILL - ALL RIGHTS RESERVED.

All rights Reserved. No part of this publication or the information in it may be quoted from or reproduced in any form by means such as printing, scanning, photocopying or otherwise without prior written permission of the copyright holder.

Disclaimer and Terms of Use: Effort has been made to ensure that the information in this book is accurate and complete, however, the author and the publisher do not warrant the accuracy of the information, text, and graphics contained within the book due to the rapidly changing nature of science, research, known and unknown facts and the internet. The Author and the publisher do not hold any responsibility for errors, omissions or contrary interpretation of the subject matter herein. This book is presented solely for motivational and informational purposes only.

Table of Contents

General Information	4
Barbados Travel Tips	6
WHERE to STAY?	7
TOP-7 Barbados Hotels	10
Car rental	15
Historical sights	17
SITES TO VISIT – Locals Advice	20
OUTDOOR ADVENTURE	26
Some popular tour operators of Barbados	31
Barbados - 100$ Trip!	32
Just 1 Amazing Day in Barbados!	34
Barbados Festivals!	37
TOP-15 Beaches of Barbados	38
10 Must Do Barbados!	50
TO TASTE	51
Shopping	54
Safety	56
Top-25 BUDGET TRAVEL TIPs	57

General Information

If you dreamed of relaxing on a paradise island lost somewhere in the seas, set out for Barbados! This small island is 34 kilometers long and 23 kilometers wide. There are many wonderful beaches here, and a part of the island is almost deserted and overgrown with rainforest.

Barbados is a state in the eastern Caribbean that is part of the British Commonwealth of Nations. The capital is the port city of Bridgetown with beautiful colonial architecture. The island is famous for beaches, botanical gardens, rum and Harrison's cave.

On the west coast, you will find prestigious hotels and golf courses. There are usually strong waves on the southeast coast, which is why beaches are popular with surfers. The rocky coast in the eastern part is suitable for hiking. The island is surrounded by coral reefs.

WHEN TO VISIT BARBADOS?

Most tourists come to Barbados from December to April. However, the weather is warm all year. The rainy season lasts from June to October, but the rains are short-term (a few minutes long) and they do not happen every day. If you are not afraid of rains, you can save a lot on the cost of traveling to Barbados during the rainy season!

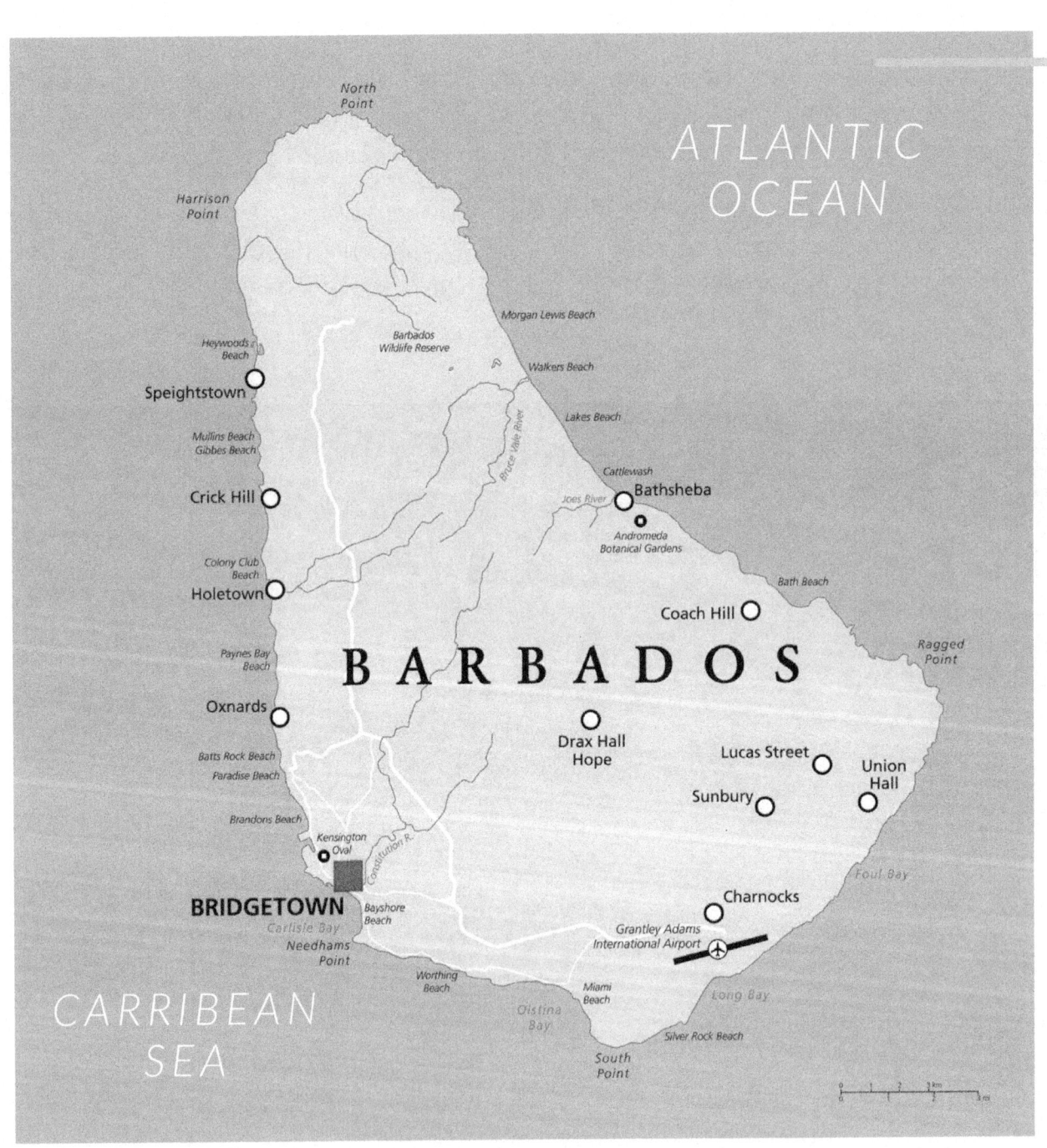

Barbados Map

Barbados Travel Tips

1. The country's monetary unit is the Barbados Dollar (BBD). 1 USD = 2 BBD, 1 EUR = 2.2 BBD.

2. Currency can be exchanged at commercial banks, exchange offices, and hotels. The most popular banks are the FirstCaribbean Bank, the Caribbean Development Bank and Scotiabank.

3. You can use the porters" services at the airport at USD 1.

4. Taxi drivers work around the clock. There are no meters, so the fare should be agreed in advance. You also need to discuss with the taxi driver in advance what currency you are paying with (USD or BBD). Buses from the airport to Bridgetown depart every 20-30 minutes, from 06:00 to 00:00. Also, there is a car rental service at the airport.

5. Buses in Barbados are state (blue ones), private (yellow ones) and minibuses (white ones). A city bus will take you anywhere on the island, and they run on schedule (from 6:00 to 21:00). The name of the final stop is indicated on the windshield of the buses. Bus stops are indicated by a red round sign with the BUS STOP inscription. The cost of the trip is USD 1 (BBD 2).

6. Windsurfers can find accommodation on the south or southeast coast of the island.

7. In most hotels and restaurants, gratuities are already included in the price of the service.

8. Most stores in the capital are open from 8:30 to 16:30 from Monday to Friday and until 13:00 on Saturday. Supermarkets are open until 20:00. The island has opened more than 1000 rum stores!

9. Local sellers often cannot find the change if you give a large USD bill, so it's better to have small notes with you.

10. Some prices: freshly prepared grilled fish in a restaurant for tourists - BBD 40-60. A bottle of water in the store - from BBD 4. A bottle of beer - from BBD 3.

11. To lower prices for excursions in Barbados, buy a special tourist passport (Heritage Barbados Passport) that costs USD 35. Two children under 12 years old can accompany passport holders free of charge. The passport allows you to visit 16 major museums and natural and architectural monuments with a 50% discount. The list includes Andromeda Botanical Gardens, Morgan Lewis Sugar Mill, St. Nicholas Abbey, Francis Plantation House, Harrison Cave, and others.

12. In Bridgetown, it is recommended to avoid the area southeast of the Farchild Street bus station around Nelson Street and Jordan Lane where red-light districts are located.

Where to Stay?

Barbados is divided into 11 districts, while there are cities in only four of them (and only villages in the rest).

CENTRAL REGIONS OF BARBADOS

- **St. Michael.** Located on the east coast, the main city of this region is the capital of Bridgetown. There are many museums and other attractions here.

- **St. James.** This region has one of four cities, Holetown. The district is located on the west coast of the island, which is its best resort!

- **St. Thomas.** Located in the center of the island.

- **St. Andrew.** The east coast region, with picturesque coastal landscapes and plenty of surfing spaces!

- **St. Joseph.** This area is home to the famous 50-acre Flower Forest botanical garden!

- **St. George.** The region has no access to the sea, but here you can find interesting sights of the colonial period.

- **St. John.** This district has unique relief. The region is also partly a site of the Andromeda Botanical Gardens created by the local botanist Iris Bannochi.

SOUTHERN BARBADOS

- **Christ Church.** This is where the city of Oistins is located. It unites many resort villages on the south coast.

- **St.Philip.** The resort district with many white-sand beaches.

NORTHERN REGIONS OF BARBADOS

- **St. Lucie.** The northern coast of Barbados is the least populated, but there are places for sports and other attractions. Here is located the famous St. Nicholas Abbey (17th century, the oldest building in Barbados) and Cherry Three Hill overgrown with relict forest.

- **St. Peter.** This area is home to the Barbados Wildlife Sanctuary where many native species of animals and plants are protected.

HOTELS IN BARBADOS: HOW AND WHERE TO CHOOSE ACCOMMODATION?

Barbados will allow any guest of the island to choose the best accommodation option without any problems: hotels and guesthouses, villas and apartments, B&B hotels.

1. Surfing, diving or snorkeling? Then choose hotels in the south, east or southeast coast of Barbados.

2. Discos and night bars? The South Coast is exactly what you need!

3. Do you prefer a relaxing holiday on the beach? Then choose the hotels of Barbados on the west coast, with golden beaches and calm sea.

4. The north of the island will suit most for those who love nature. This is an island reserve.

5. For lovers of wild places, the east coast is exactly what you need: there are few tourists, and wild beaches are very picturesque.

The most expensive hotels are located in the west. The south of the island is suitable for those who are looking for cheaper accommodation.

HOTEL PRICES

Cost of living in hotels of Barbados:

- **5*** Hilton Barbados or Coral Reef Club hotels - a double room costs USD 200 - 400

- **3*** - 4*Hotels - South Beach Hotel, Coral Sands Resort or Sugar Bay Barbados - a double room costs USD 120 - 200. However, you can find a 3* hotel worth USD 60 - 90

- **Renting an apartment or room** at the B&B hotel costs USD 80 - 130 per day

- **Villa rental** - USD 200 - 600 per day

Coral Reef Club

TOP-7 Barbados Hotels

1. ST PETER'S BAY LUXURY RESORT AND RESIDENCIES

2. WAVES HOTEL AND SPA BY ELEGANT HOTELS

3. SUGAR BAY BARBADOS

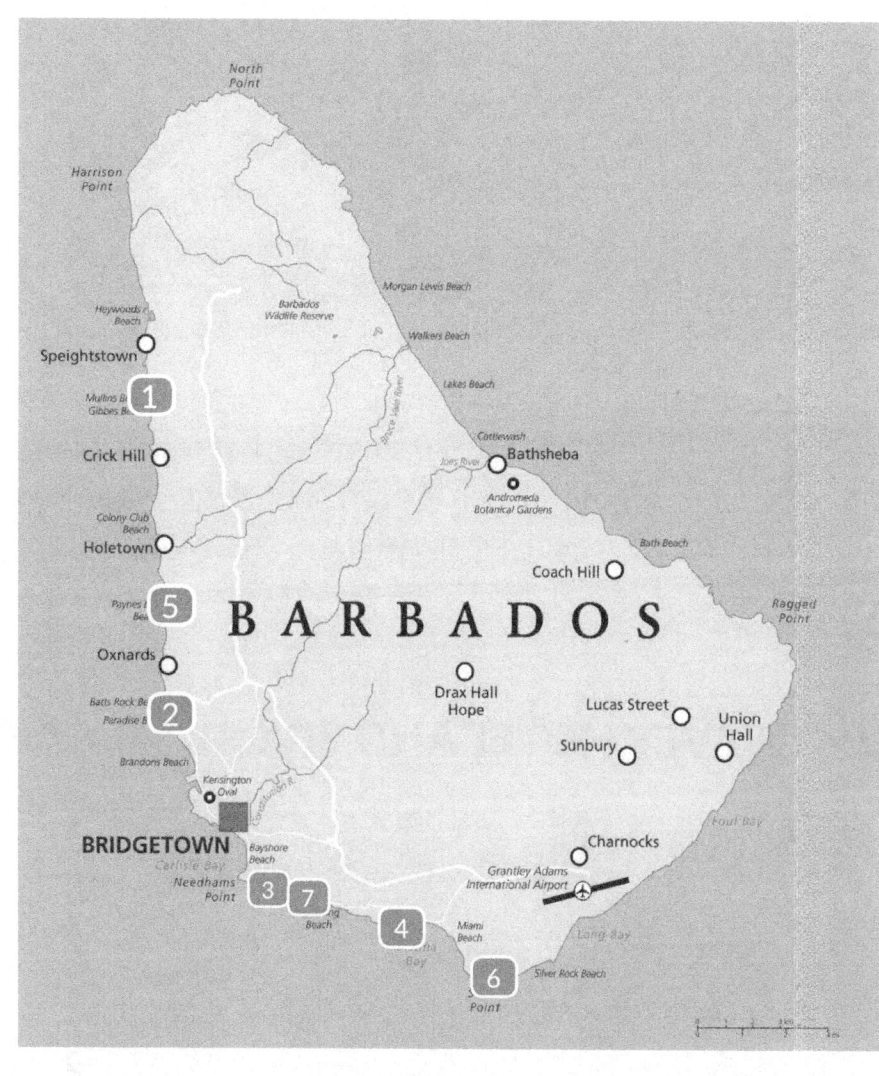

4. BOUGAINVILLEA BARBADOS

5. TAMARIND BY ELEGANT HOTELS

6. LITTLE ARCHES BOUTIQUE HOTEL - ADULTS ONLY

7. THE SOCO HOTEL - ALL INCLUSIVE - ADULTS ONLY

1. ST PETER'S BAY LUXURY RESORT AND RESIDENCIES

☆ ☆ ☆ ☆ ☆

- **Price:** € 503
- **Beach:** A perfectly clean beach with snow-white fine sand. The shallow water area is 15-25 meters. There are zones with stones and corals; there are almost no waves near the coast.
- **Description:** Luxury apartments for families or friends. The territory is small, with outdoor pools, flowerbeds and palm trees. The rooms offer a magnificent view of the sea, a terrace and a private kitchen in each room. Guests can take advantage of a fitness room, spa, and water sports equipment. You can go on a boat trip or take a water taxi to any part on the coast.

2. WAVES HOTEL AND SPA BY ELEGANT HOTELS

☆ ☆ ☆ ☆

- **Price:** € 313
- **Beach:** The beach is clean, the entrance to the water is gentle. You can snorkel on site and watch the sea turtles and octopuses. The shallow water area is large, waves occur in the afternoon.
- **Description:** a luxurious hotel with a large territory and polite staff. Suitable for a quiet holiday. In the evenings, the hotel's restaurants play live music. In the hotel, you can take advantage of a restaurant, a garden, a spa, a fitness center, water skiing, yachts, surfing and boat trips.

3. SUGAR BAY BARBADOS

☆ ☆ ☆ ☆

- **Price:** € 207
- **Beach:** The fine white sand of the beach is interspersed with coral chips; rubber-bathing shoes are needed. There are no big waves. A large area of shallow water.

- **Description:** The hotel is designed for newlyweds, couples and senior citizens who value privacy and tranquility. It offers a restaurant, swimming pool, car rental, cinema, library, windsurfing and diving equipment rental, and spa. For holidaymakers, hiking and field trips are organized.

4. BOUGAINVILLEA BARBADOS

☆ ☆ ☆ ☆

- **Price:** € 154
- **Beach:** A wide beach of white fine sand with a large area of shallow water. Great conditions for young children. Small waves make it possible to surf.

- **Description:** Elegant hotel with the luxurious design of the territory and a pool bar. Each room has its balcony and terrace. There is a games room for children, a fitness room for adults. If you wish, you can visit the nearby Graham Hall Nature Reserve or have fun at the St. Lawrence Gap nightclubs which are just a 5-minute drive away.

5. TAMARIND BY ELEGANT HOTELS

- **Price:** € 175

- **Beach:** Sandy beach with a large area of shallow water. Stones and shards of coral can be found in the water, so rubber shoes are required. You can snorkel in the area surrounded by rare fish and sea turtles.

- **Description:** The hotel has a small area with a pool and a garden. You can go water skiing and canoeing, go sailing in the ocean, and rent equipment for surfing and snorkeling. The hotel has a fitness center, spa, children's playroom, billiards club and tennis court.

6. LITTLE ARCHES BOUTIQUE HOTEL - ADULTS ONLY

- **Price:** € 229

- **Beach:** A beach of fine white sand with a gentle entrance to the water. Shards of coral can be found in the water, so it is better to swim in special shoes. High and low tides are insignificant.

- **Description:** This small hotel is a 5-minute drive from Bridgetown. There are concierge services and a spa center here.

7. THE SOCO HOTEL - ALL INCLUSIVE - ADULTS ONLY

- **Price:** € 300
- **Beach:** A narrow sandy beach is located in a small bay. The coast on both sides of the beach is covered with large stones. The entrance to the water is convenient, high and low tides are insignificant.
- **Description:** The hotel accepts adults only. It features an outdoor pool and spa. You can rent a bike. Surf and sailing enthusiasts can go to Silver Sands Beach 5 minutes from the hotel.

Car Rental

To rent a car in Barbados, you will need an international driver's license, and besides it, registration of local license (this costs USD 5). The driver must be at least 21 and no more than 70 years old. Car rental costs USD 90-120 per day. The cost of a liter of gasoline in Barbados is BBD 1 (USD 0.5). There are toll roads in Barbados you can find out about at a car rental company.

WHERE TO RENT:

- Stoutes Car Rental Ltd
- Drive-A-Matic Car Rentals
- Bajan Car Rentals
- Courtesy Rent A Car
- Orange Smile Car Trawler

SPEED LIMITS AT BARBADOS:

- in the city - 30-40 km / h
- out of town - 60 km / h
- on the highway - 80 km / h

RULES OF THE ROAD IN BARBADOS:

- Left-hand traffic. Overtaking is allowed only on the right side.
- The dipped headlights must be switched on in the evening and at night.
- The driver and all passengers must wear seat belts. There are no specific rules regarding the carriage of small children in a car.
- It is forbidden to talk on a cell phone while driving.
- The permissible level of alcohol in the driver's blood is 0.5 ppm.

PENALTIES FOR TRAFFIC VIOLATIONS:

- Parking on the sites for disabled people - about USD 25
- Speeding - from USD 70
- Red-light running - within USD 50
- Unfastened seat belt - about USD 50
- Movement on a roadside - USD 450

TAXI. Always negotiate with the driver in advance about the price! Here are some phone numbers for calling a taxi:

- MHKK Tours & Taxi Service (+1 246-252-0083)
- Sun Tours Barbados (+1 246-434-8430)
- A Plus Tours and Events Barbados (+1 246-284-2411)
- Sam's Tours & Taxi Services (+1 246-433-9248)

Historical Sights

ST. JOHN'S PARISH CHURCH

 St. John, Barbados  6:00 – 18:00 (Daily)  Free

A historic church in Barbados with gorgeous east coast views built in 1846! Gothic style architecture and tropical garden.

St. John's Parish Church

GEORGE WASHINGTON HOUSE

 George Washington House, The Garrison, St. Michael

 9:00 – 16:30 (Sun - close)

 Tour George Washington house + the Garrison tunnels – $15 and $7.5 (children 5-12)

19 year-old George Washington and his brother spent 2 months at this old house in 1751. Barbados is the only foreign land George ever visited!

PARLIAMENT BUILDINGS

 Parliament Square, Bridgetown

 10:00 – 16:00 (Sun, Tue – close)

 $5

Parliament Building is the most famous city landmark in Bridgetown. Neo-gothic style architecture, an old clock tower, and a balcony at the top. You can visit the museum of Parliament and the National Heroes Gallery.

NATIONAL HEROES SQUARE

 High and Trafalgar Streets, Bridgetown

 daily

 free

National Heroes Square (or Trafalgar Square) is located in the center of Bridgetown, close to the Parliament Buildings and cruise terminal. The Square contains three main memorials: an obelisk dated 1925, a statue of Admiral Nelson and a Dolphin Fountain. There are many shops and restaurants in this area.

GUN HILL SIGNAL STATION

 Hwy. 4

 9:00 – 17:00 (Daily). Suggested duration: 1-2 hours.

 $6 ($3 for children under 12)

National Heroes Square (or Trafalgar Square) is located in the center of Bridgetown, close to the Parliament Buildings and cruise terminal. The Square contains three main memorials: an obelisk dated 1925, a statue of Admiral Nelson and a Dolphin Fountain. There are many shops and restaurants in this area.

Gun Hill Signal Station

Sites to Visit - Locals Advice

MORGAN LEWIS SUGAR MILL 1727

 Morgan Lewis    10:00 – 17:00 (daily)    $5 (guided tour). Grounds and Cafe – free.

This is an unique place with a history of 250 years! If you take a guided tour, you will learn a lot about the processing of sugarcane, technology, and history of this craft. There is also a great cafe where you can drink perhaps the best coffee on the island! And be sure to take a selfie against the background of the mill!

Morgan Lewis Sugar Mill 1727

CHAMBERLAIN BRIDGE AND INDEPENDENCE ARCH

 Bridgetown    daily    free

This is one of Bridgetown's main attractions. Here you can take a walk, do some shopping, and take a selfie for the memory! It is especially beautiful here in the evening when the arch and the bridge are illuminated.

THE SPEIGHTSTOWN MURAL

 Queen's Street, Speightstown    daily    free

I don't think you need to specifically go to this place to see this mural, but if you are on the way - it's worth it! This is a bright fresco on the wall where you can get excellent photos for memory. There is also a beach nearby.

The Speightstown Mural

HP BATIK STUDIO

 No. 2 Edge Hill Heights, St. Thomas

 9:00 – 17:00 (Sun – close)

 visit free. Workshop – depends on activity.

Have you dreamed of becoming an artist? Think you don't know how to draw pictures? This is not true! You are a true artist and you will see this at the master class!

In this art studio, you can buy paintings or draw them yourself (it takes 6 hours). There is also a unique clothing store and a good Tree House restaurant here.

BAXTER'S ROAD

 Bridgetown

 daily

 free

If you have a couple of hours to walk around the city, then go to Baxter's Road. Here you will find bright colors buildings, many shops, the best-fried fish, and a colorful street market. Also, you may come to this place late at night (after 22:00) and see Bridgetown's night-life!

PETREA GARDEN

 Trents, Bridgetown

 9:00 – 17:00 (daily)

 free

If you want to relax in a beautiful garden among tropical plants where there are few people, then go to this garden for 1-2 hours. You should not go here by making it a special trip, but if you are there, you will like it!

CODRINGTON COLLEGE

 Sargeant Street

 9:00 – 18:00 (Daily)

 $5 (self-guided historic, architectural or natural tour) or 2.5$ (play-park, picnic areas)

Codrington College is the oldest theological college in the western hemisphere! You can find beautifully landscaped grounds, historic buildings with pretty architecture and a large lily pond.

Codrington College

FOURSQUARE RUM DISTILLERY

 Hwy 6, Foursquare St Philip    9:00 – 16:30 (Mon – Fri). Suggested duration: 2 hours.    rum tasting $10

You can come here on your own and buy a rum tasting ticket on site. There is also a beautiful garden and souvenir shops.

ST NICHOLAS ABBEY

 St. Nicholas Abbey, Cherry Tree Hill, St. Peter    9:00 – 16:30 (Sun - Fri). Guided tours from 10:30 – 15:30. Suggested duration: 3 hours.

- Entrance with an hourly tour – $23 (kids 5-12 - $10)
- Heritage Railway – $30 (kids 3-11 - $15)

What you will see: the old house, bottling plant and syrup factory, museum, plantation's gardens and a breathtaking view of the east coast! Also, you will have a complimentary rum or punch (or rum tasting)!

One of the newest attractions at St. Nicholas Abbey is the Heritage Railway! A one-hour round trip includes: Great House, wild fowl lake, mature mahogany woodlands and Cherry Tree Hill.

Also, you can enjoy a lunch, tea or coffee at the Terrace Café.

St Nicholas Abbey

«TIYI BY DESIGN» ART JEWELRY STUDIO

 Store No. 12, Town Square mall, Speightstown

 10:00 – 17:00 (Tue – Fri), 10:00 – 14:00 (Sat)

 free

This is an exclusive Caribbean art jewelry brand, handmade and individually designed. In the workshop you can see how the craftsmen work and make a piece of jewelry yourself! Must visit for girls!

«Tiyi By Design» Art Jewelry Studio

Outdoor Adventure

HARRISON'S CAVE

LOCATION: Welchman Hall, St. Thomas, Barbados

- Tram-tour: daily 8:45 - 15:45 pm (tour duration: 1 hour)
- Eco-adventure tour: daily at 9:00 and 12:00 (tour duration: 3 hour)
- Walk in cave: every last Saturday of each month

- Tram-tour: adults $30 and children $15
- Eco-adventure tour: $100 (by reservation only)
- Walk in cave: adults $20 and children $10

This is the largest of the caves of Barbados, and there is a whole gallery of stalactites and stalagmites there. This is one of the few caves in the world where you can take a tram! During the tour, you will learn the history of the cave and take stunning photos. It is easily accessible from any hotel, and you can buy a tour at the cave box office.

Harrison's Cave

ANDROMEDA BOTANIC GARDENS

 Bathsheba, St Joseph    9:00 – 16:30 (daily)    $15 (children – free)

Local botanist, Iris Bannochi, created botanical gardens on the east coast of Barbados. This is a tropical garden with a unique collection of plants! Also, you can find animals and birds here. You seem to be in another world of wildlife! A truly amazing place!

FARLEY HILL NATIONAL PARK

 Highway 2, Benny Hall    9:00 – 16:30 (daily)    $5

Here you will find a magnificent park and picturesque ruins of Sunbury Plantation House. You seem to fall into the past - a plantation house, magnificent views, lush green plants ... Everything speaks about the history of the island. A unique place!

GARRISON SAVANNAH - BARBADOS TURF CLUB

 The Garrison, St Micheal    depends on Race Calendar    from $5 (depends on the area)

Are you a gambler? Then you definitely need to visit this place! A great atmosphere, easy to put a bet on (minimum bet $1), drinks and a lot of fun! You can also visit horse training and even chat with their trainers!

Barbados Turf Club

PEG FARM *SPECIAL MISSION!*

 Easy Hall Plantation, Easy Hall    8:00 – 16:30 (daily)   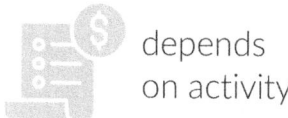 depends on activity

This is the best place for kids! However, it will be interesting for adults as well! What does it have for you?

- **Tours:** Sunrise on the East Side (3 hours, $50-75), Island Nature Experience (4 hours, $55-80) and Tea Time (3 hours, $50-65). During the tours, you can get closer to nature and animals!

- **Café:** Chicken & Papaya Salad, Raised and Braised Hen, Pulled Pork Papaya Pancakes and more! All cooking products are natural and locally grown.

- **Camping:** you can spend the night at the campsite, which is comfortably equipped ($30/1 night/1 person).

PEG Farm

KENSINGTON OVAL

 President Kennedy Dr, Bridgetown    9:00 – 15:30 (Sun, Sat - close)    depends on event

This is the oldest cricket ground in Barbados (1881). I highly recommend visiting this place, even if there is no cricket competition. It is an amazing modern architecture. You can visit the cricket ground during the tour.

BARBADOS POLO CLUB

 Holders Hill    8:00 – 15:00    depends on activity (from $10)

It's very exciting to watch a polo game! But you need to understand the rules of the game and what is happening on the field. Also, there is an equipped bar, food and drinks are available. You will definitely like this place!

Barbados Polo Club

ISLAND SAFARI

 Barbados (call +1-246-429-5337)  daily  $25 - 65 (4-hour jeep tour)

During the tour you will drive half of the island! You will see Gun Hill Signal Station, Andrew's Factory, Parris Hill, Bathsheba Park, Foster Hall, Andromeda Gardens and much more! Also, you will have a photo and lunch stops (3 times). There are several options for the tour (different routes and duration of the trip). You can also order a personal tour!

Island Safari

KENDAL SPORTING BARBADOS

 Carrington, St. Philip  11:00 – 17:00 (Mon – close)  depends on activity (from $10)

The following activities are offered here: shooting ranges, water balloons war, archery, fishing, rapid paintball, canoeing! Therefore, it will be fun for both adults and children!

BARBADOS MINI GOLF CLUB

 24, Cane Garden Heights, White Hall, St. Thomas  14:00 – 20:00 (Thu, Sun), 14:00 – 22:00 (Fri, Sat). Close – Mon, Tue, Wed

 $5 - children, $7.5 - adult

This golf club is perfect for children. They will really like it here! A professional coach works with the children. Adults can relax in the club bar.

Some popular tour operators of Barbados

1. **ISLAND SAFARI**
   - **Activity:** Jeep Safari Tours
   - **Location:** pickup from your hotel (call at +1-246-429-5337)

2. **EL TIGRE CATAMARAN SAILING CRUISES**
   - **Activity:** Boat Tours, Water Sports, Animals
   - **Location:** Steel Building, Cavans Lane, Bridgetown (8:00 – 18:00)

3. **ELEGANCE CATAMARAN CRUISES**
   - **Activity:** Boat Tours, Water Sports, Animals
   - **Location:** Bridgetown (call at +1-246-830-4218)

4. **CALABAZA SAILING CRUISES**
   - **Activity:** Boat Tours, Water Sports, Animals
   - **Location:** Bridgetown (call at +1-246-826-4048)

5. **ACTION CHARTERS**
   - **Activity:** Boat Tours, Water Sports, Outdoor activity, Animals
   - **Location:** Aberfoyle, Maxwell Main Road, Christ Church (call at +1-246-231-1234)

Barbados - 100$ Trip!

2 DAYS / 1 NIGHT. BUDGET – 100$

DAY 1

- **9:00.** Grantley Adams International Airport Barbados - Bridgetown. Travel by bus - $1. Duration: 30 min.
- **10:00.** Walk in the center of the city - the embankment, the Parliament building and the bridge.
- **13:00.** Find the nearest bus stop and head to Dover Beach (fare $1).
- **13:30.** Rent a surf on Dover Beach -at $20 (half a day), and move on to the waves! The waves here are calm and perfect for beginners. Surfing is very cool!

- **16:30.** And now go to the most popular city beach, Pebble Beach (fare $1). Here you can have a bite in a cafe: sandwich + juice ($10). There are many tourists here and you can make friends with people from all over the world!
- **19:30.** Dinner at the coastal cafe: grilled fish + tea ($11).
- **21:30.** Spend the night on the beach (in a tent or hammock) or rent the most inexpensive hotel at $30-40.

DAY 2

- **8:00.** Wake up and into the sea! In the morning, you can see little turtles on Pebble Beach! You can play with them and help them crawl to the water.

- **10:00.** The most delicious food is street food! Near the Pebble Beach there is a Cuz Fish eatery, Fish Stand (a small blue stall). Try a fish burger at $5.

- **11:00.** Go to Bathsheba Beach (fare $1). There are no people here, a light wind is blowing from the sea, and you will find green palm trees and stone blocks of bizarre shapes here. This place is perfect for privacy, just relax and enjoy the ocean! In a roadside cafe, take a serving of shrimp and coffee ($8).

- **13:00.** Did you have a good rest? Then head to the north of the island, to the Ultimate Flower Cave. The fare costs $2. This is an amazing cave with access to the ocean!

Just 1 Amazing Day in Barbados!

You have only 1 day and you have a car. Then this amazing independent tour is just for you!

1. BOTTOM BAY - THE BEACH, THE MOST BEAUTIFUL VIEWS OF THE OCEAN.

 all day    free    1 hour

2. THE PARLIAMENT BUILDING - ARCHITECTURE, HISTORY.

 *Travel by car - 40 min.*

 all day    free    1 hour

The Parliament Building

3. CARLISLE BAY - THE BEACH, DIVING WITH TURTLES!

 On foot - 10 min.

 all day    free    1.5 hours.

4. ATLANTIS SUBMARINE BARBADOS - DIVING!

 *Travel by car - 15 min.*

 8:00 - 16:00 (Sun - close).    from $50    1 hour.

Atlantis Submarine Barbados - diving

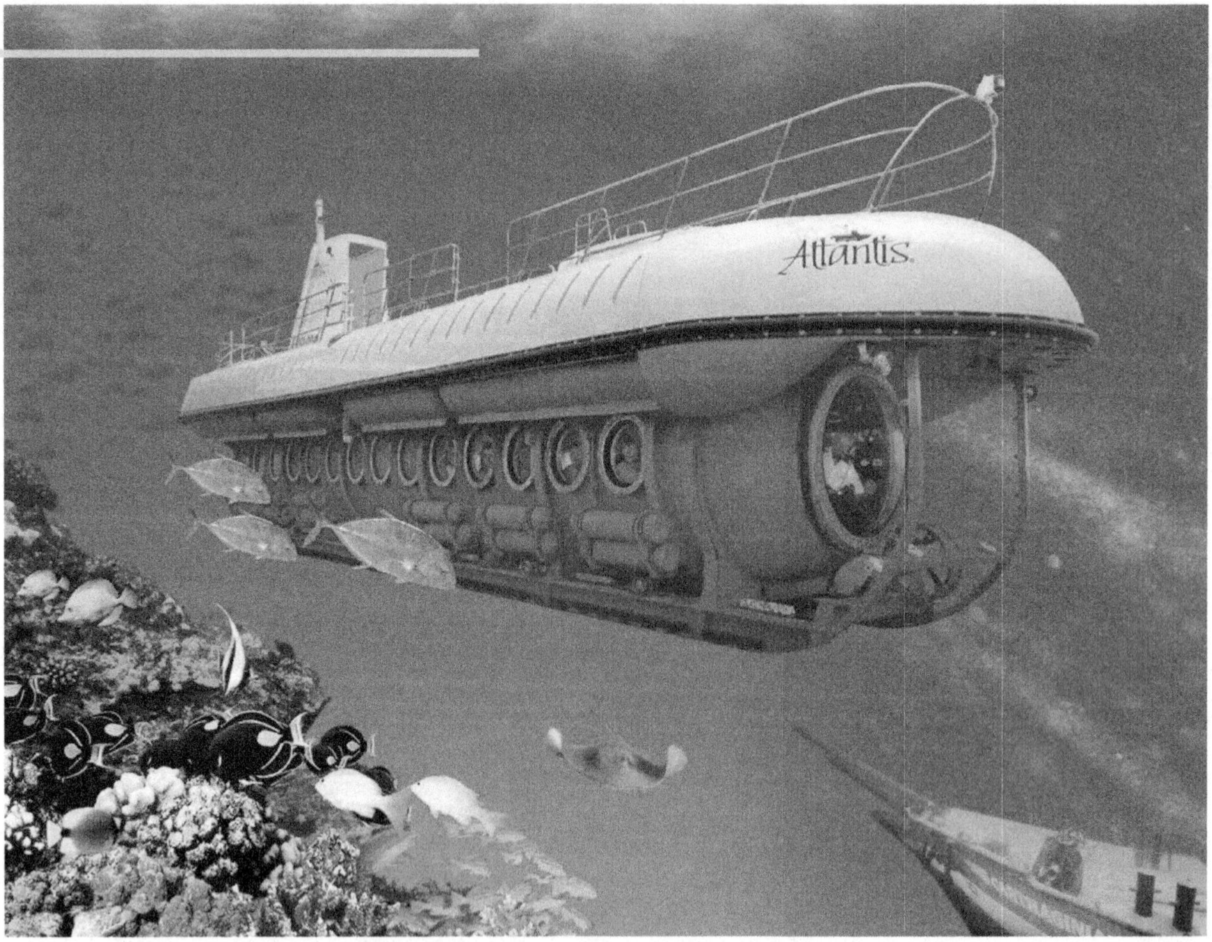

5. PAYNES PAY BEACH - BEACH, SNORKELING.

 *Travel by car -20 min.*

 all day    free    1.5 hours

6. HARRISONS CAVE - A LIMESTONE CAVE WITH WATERFALLS, LAKES, STALACTITES AND A SIGHTSEEING TRAM.

 *Travel by car -20 min.*

 all day    from $20    2.5 hours

Barbados Festivals!

- **January 1** - New Year
- **February** - Competitions for the International Polo Challenge Cup
- **March** - Congaline Street Festival
- **March** - St. Lawrence Craft and Food Exhibition
- **March** - Classical Music Festival
- **March** - Race for the Sandy Line Cup
- **March** - Holders-Season Classic Art Festival
- **May** - Barbados Assembly Carnival
- **May** - gospels music festival
- **August** - Crop Over Carnival (a dance carnival with alcohol)
- **October** - Barbados International Triathlon
- **November** - National Independent Festival of Creativity and Art
- **November** - Caribbean surfing championship in Betsheb
- **November** - Chefs from all over the world come to Barbados to participate in the Food, Wine and Rum Festival
- **November 20** - National Fun Walk Folk Festival
- **December** - Race of the "Roads of Barbados" series
- **December** - Run Barbados Cultural Festival

TOP-15 Beaches of Barbados

THE COAST OF BARBADOS

The south coast is the meeting point of the Caribbean Sea and the Atlantic Ocean with ideal conditions for windsurfing. Along the coast, there are small 3* and 4* hotels, bars, restaurants, and discos. The center of nightlife is the town of St. Lawrence Gap.

The west coast is washed by the Caribbean Sea and is famous for its golden sandy beaches and calm clear waters. The best hotels on the island, located right here, are suitable for relaxing holiday lovers. You can spend evenings in cozy restaurants and bars.

The eastern coast of Barbados is washed by the Atlantic Ocean. This is the most beautiful part of the island, but there are few tourists here. It has excellent surfing conditions and wild beaches.

The north of Barbados is the least populated area. Here you will find the Barbados Wildlife Sanctuary in St. Peter County (25 km north of Bridgetown), where you can see green monkeys, roe deer, otters, turtles, and other exotic animals and birds.

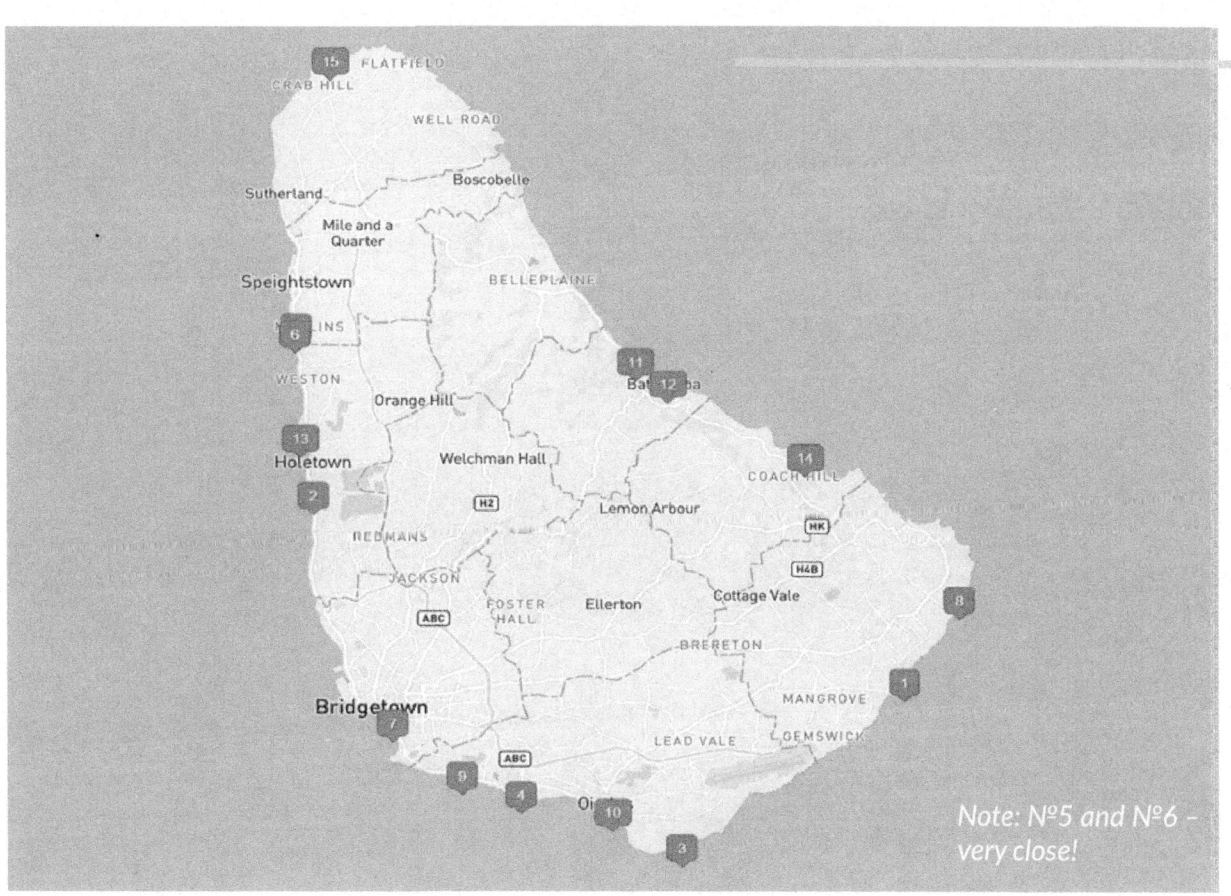

Map of Beaches of Barbados

Note: №5 and №6 – very close!

1. CRANE BEACH

Crane Beach is a picturesque site located in the bay in the southeastern part of the island. It constantly falls into the top ten most beautiful coasts in the world! Crane Beach is a long and wide sandy beach with very soft sand of a pink hue that looks like powder. Around the beach there are limestone cliffs, tropical vegetation and coconut palms. Couples, celebrities, and surfers come here. Both medium and high waves form here. Coastal waters are surrounded by a coral reef. This is a public beach, but there are few tourists here.

INFRASTRUCTURE

The most convenient place to stay is Crane Residential Resort. This is the oldest resort hotel in Barbados built in 1867.

- Rental of umbrellas and sun loungers (free for hotel guests). No rental of surfboards (even at the hotel).
- Showers and toilets function during the season, and the beach is controlled by patrolmen and lifeguards.
- On the shore, there are picnic tables, a kiosk with drinks and various goods. Bike rental is available for riding tours.

Crane Beach

2. SANDY LANE BAY

Sandy Lane Bay is often visited by world-class celebrities, so you can get photos with them! The beach is located on the west coast of Barbados, in a quiet bay. It is a long and wide beach. at the approach to the sea is gentle and safe for children. On weekdays, the beach is almost empty, but there are many tourists here at weekends.

INFRASTRUCTURE

The beach is located next to the Sandy Lane Hotel Resort (1933).
- Rent of umbrellas and sun loungers
- Water sports activities: water skiing, diving, snorkeling, sea fishing, boating and jet skiing.
- There is a bar on the beach. The nearest cafes and restaurants are located in the neighboring Holtown. You can buy products in the mall (near the beach).

HELPFUL INFORMATION

- You can get to the beach by public transport from Holtown.
- Access to the beach is possible only from the south side.
- Between July and October, Hawksbill turtles nest on the beach.

Sandy Lane Bay

3. SILVER SANDS

Located in the southern part of the island, next to South Point Lighthouse. The total length of the sandy coast is 0.5 km. The beach consists of two bays. The western part is suitable for a relaxing holiday, the eastern one - for lovers of extreme water sports (the wind is stable here). There are few people here on weekdays. At weekends, the place is crowded with lovers of extreme water sports. The beach is not controlled by lifeguards!

INFRASTRUCTURE

HELPFUL INFORMATION

2 km from the beach - Moon Raker Beach Hotel and Inchcape Seaside Villa.
- No rental of sun loungers or umbrellas.
- There is a club for surfers on the coast in which you can take a training course and rent equipment.
- Bring food and drinks with you. There are picnic tables on the shore, as well as a children's playground.

- You can easily get to the beach from the capital of the island by public buses.
- You can find a great spot where you can swim with turtles 3 km north of the beach.
- A trip to the beach can be combined with a visit to the historic South Point Lighthouse and the fishing village of Oistins. If you travel with children, you can visit the Barbados Nature Reserve.

Silver Sands

4. DOVER

Dover Beach is a beautiful beach in the bay, on the outskirts of the town of Oistins on the south coast of Barbados. Dover Beach is not suitable for families with children as there are a lot of youth and parties here.

The coastal area of the beach is covered with light sand and planted with trees that form a natural shadow. It is often windy on the beach, which creates weak and medium waves. The winter-spring period is suitable for windsurfing, surfing, Hobie Cat sailing.

INFRASTRUCTURE

HELPFUL INFORMATION

- Along Dover Beach, there are a lot of restaurants and bars, discos, souvenir shops, a cricket ground, football and basketball pitches.
- In the beach area, you can rent sun loungers and other equipment, pleasure boats and boats, catamarans and jet skis.
- There is a rescue service.

- You can get to the beach from the nearest town of Oistins in 10 minutes by taxi or on foot.

Dover

5. MULLINS BEACH

Mullins Beach is a beach located in a bay on the northwest coast of Barbados, 15 km from Bridgetown. The coastal strip of the beach is covered with white sand, the entrance to the water is gentle, the seabed is sandy, and there are no large waves or dangerous undercurrents.

INFRASTRUCTURE

- The beach area is equipped with showers, toilets, sunbeds and tents.
- There are several bars and restaurants near the coastal area. There are also several playgrounds and attractions for children.
- There is no rescue service on the beach.

HELPFUL INFORMATION

- You can get to the beach by taxi or bus to Speightstown. There is a parking lot near the beach.

Mullins Beach

6. GIBBES BEACH

Gibbes Beach is a cozy beach about 500 m long. It is located on the west coast, a 5-minute walk from Mullins Bay Beach. The entrance to the sea is sharp and deep! The beach is ideal for secluded relaxation lovers. Sometimes Gibbes Beach is chosen for a stop during boat cruises. There are Holetown and Speightstown near the beach where there are many restaurants, bars and shops.

INFRASTRUCTURE

- There are no amenities on the beach
- You need to take food and drinks with you.

HELPFUL INFORMATION

- You can get to the beach by car or bus, walk a little along the path directly to the beach.

7. BROWNES BEACH

Brownes Beach is one of the largest beaches in Barbados located a 10-minute walk from the center of Bridgetown. This is a wide strip of white sand in Carlisle Bay. The sea in the area is clean and calm, ideal for families with young children. There are sunken ships in the bay, which is very interesting for scuba diving.

INFRASTRUCTURE

- Rental of umbrellas and sunbeds, toilets, bars.
- You can book boat excursions around the bay and fishing tours here.
- Rescue service is operating.
- Parking is available near the beach.

Brownes Beach

8. BOTTOM BAY

Bottom Bay is one of the most picturesque secluded beaches of Barbados. It is located in a bay on the southeastern edge of the island. There are rocks around the beach.

Large sea turtles and whales sometimes appear here. Swimming at high and medium waves is not recommended. There may be strong undercurrents, and the beach is not controlled by lifeguards!

INFRASTRUCTURE

HELPFUL INFORMATION

- There is parking for cars, and you have to go down the rocky steps to get to the coast.
- The nearest cafe and restaurant is a 30-minute walk from here.
- There is only wildlife here. There are no bars with food or drink on the beach.
- There are no toilets or showers on the beach.
- It is most crowded at weekends (there may be traders renting sun loungers).

You can stay at the Tropical Winds Hotel or the Crane Resort Hotel.

- A rest in Bottom Bay may be combined with visiting attractions: south of this beach, you can see Cave Bay and Crane Beach. North of the bay, there is East Point and Radjed Point lighthouses and Palmetto Bay.

Mullins Beach

9. ACCRA (ROCKLEY) BEACH

Accra (Rockley) Beach is a long sandy beach located in the southern part of the island. Accra Beach has the natural shade of trees. Stable moderate wave strength is excellent for fans of windsurfing and surfing. The southern part of the beach with the shallow coastal strip of the sea and sandy bottom is suitable for a beach holiday with children.

INFRASTRUCTURE

- Sun loungers, beach and sporting goods and equipment rental, water rides.
- Restaurants and bars, souvenir shops.

HELPFUL INFORMATION

- You can get to Accra Beach by car or by bus. Car park and a bus stop are located next to the beach.

10. ENTERPRISE BEACH

Enterprise Beach is a beach area near the town of Oistins. It consists of two sections, the northern (Enterprise Beach) and the southern (Miami Beach) surrounded by cliffs.

The beach is suitable for families with small children. The coast is gentle, the sea is shallow, and the waves are very small. Enterprise (Miami) Beach is ideal for jogging and walking.

INFRASTRUCTURE

- Rescue service available.
- Rental of sun loungers and umbrellas.
- Near the beach, there is a bar, beach shopping complex and a picnic area.

HELPFUL INFORMATION

- A fish festival is held at Oistins every April, during which shows and fishing competitions are held.

11. CATTLEWASH BEACH

Cattlewash Beach is a rocky beach on the east coast near Bathsheb. The site is not intended for swimming! But it is suitable for ecotourism and photo shoots. The beach is covered with yellow-orange sand, there are scattered fragments of snags of trees thrown ashore by storms. The beach is considered one of the longest ones in Barbados. There are often stormy winds here that can occur suddenly, very high waves and strong coastal currents.

 **INFRASTRUCTURE**

 **HELPFUL INFORMATION**

- There are villas on the coast of Cattlewash that are rented to tourists during the summer. Closest to the beach is the Atlantis Historic Inn located in a historic building in the fishing village of Tent Bay.
- There are no shops or bars on the coast (bring food and water with you).
- There are no toilets or showers on the beach.
- At weekends, the coast is controlled by lifeguards

- You can get there by car or on foot from the town of Bathsheb.
- You can visit the Andromeda Gardens and Barclays Park in this region.

Cattlewash Beach

12. BATHSHEBA BEACH

Bathsheba Beach is a large sandy and rocky beach. It is located near the village of Virsavia, on the east coast of the island. The visiting card of the beach is a large boulder located in the coastal strip of the beach.

The area has strong waves, which is great for surfers. Every year, the International Pro Surfing Classic Surfing Championships are held here. The Bathsheba Beach area is ideal for picnics and hiking. Due to strong waves, rocky bottom and tides it is not recommended to swim here!

HELPFUL INFORMATION

- You can get to Bathsheba Beach from Bridgetown in 40-60 minutes by car, taxi or bus. There are several restaurants and shops, as well as hotels and guesthouses where you can rent housing near the beach.

13. FOLKESTONE BEACH

Folkestone Beach is a cozy calm beach for families and picnics located on the Caribbean coast. There is a sunken ship in the bay. You can rent a boat with a transparent bottom for diving and rent diving equipment.

INFRASTRUCTURE

- Rescue service available.
- Rental of sun loungers and umbrellas, parking, showers, toilets.
- There is a Marine Park with aquariums and a museum near the beach.
- Basketball and playgrounds, tennis courts.

HELPFUL INFORMATION

- You can get to the beach from Bridgetown by bus or car.

14. BATH BEACH

Bath Beach is located on the Atlantic coast, in the eastern part of Barbados. It is a convenient place for picnics and family walks, safe for swimming. During low tide, the reef rises above the surface of the water, which allows you to explore it even on foot; the main thing is to wear beach shoes.

 ### INFRASTRUCTURE

 ### HELPFUL INFORMATION

- Rescue service available.
- There are showers and toilets
- Car parking.

- Here you can walk to a small waterfall located north of the beach, go fishing or collecting shells. If you come here for a picnic, it is better to take food with you.

15. ARCHER'S BAY

Archer's Bay is a secluded small beach in Archer Bay with cliffs around. It is located on the northwest coast, 25 km from Bridgetown.

There are a lot of dangerous underwater currents and stones, as well as coral reefs in this area, so it is unsafe to swim in Archer's Bay! There is no infrastructure on the beach. It is great for a romantic picnic and photoshoot.

 ### HELPFUL INFORMATION

- You can only get to the beach by car and then go down the cliff using a steep path. A trip here is combined with a visit to the Animal Flower Cave. You can rent a house in the town of Cluffs (there are cafes, bars, souvenir shops and other shops here).

10 Must Do Barbados!

1. Swim in the Atlantic Ocean!
2. Visit St. Michael's Cathedral where George Washington himself prayed!
3. Play cricket or golf!
4. Go to the racetrack and bet on some horse!
5. Take a surf ride on the waves of the Caribbean!
6. Ride along the coast of the island!
7. Go down to the Harrison Caves!
8. Go scuba diving to the coral reefs of Barbados!
9. See unique monuments to colonial sugar plantations!
10. Order flying fish and sea urchins at restaurants!

To Taste

Seafood. Porridge made of grain and caviar and flying fish of all kinds are the most common dishes of Barbados. Also, you can eat sea urchin, lobster, shrimp, dorado, mackerel, tuna, shark and barracuda, as well as various shells.

Vegetables, root crops, and fruits. In Barbados, yams, eggplant, sweet potatoes, cassava, breadfruit, avocados, green banana, guava, cherries, oranges, Indian dates, sugar apples (the most expensive fruit on the island) are grown and eaten.

Pork. This is the most popular meat in Barbados. I especially recommend trying Pepperpot or Kohoblopot, spiced meat stewed with okra.

TOP-5 DISHES TO TRY

- Flying fish, a symbol of the Caribbean island of Barbados. Burgers with flying fish are especially delicious. To do this, fish are cleaned of bones and deep-fried. Served on a bun with salad and sauce of your choice.

- Roti is a tortilla in which boiled potatoes are wrapped, mixed with meat stewed in curry sauce. I advise you to buy in a chain of Chefette fast-food restaurants.

- Breadfruit (this is a side dish). It is baked, cut and served with fried ribs or baked meat with spicy bajan pepper sauce.

- Lobsters, shrimp tuna and mahi-mahi steaks, parrotfish, sea bass and other seafood does not cost much! Where to buy: at the Oistins fish market before 2 p.m.

- Cou-cou, coo-coo or fungi is a dish in the form of porridge made of cornmeal and shrimp. It has a very specific taste!

WHAT TO DRINK ON BARBADOS

- RUM. But it is not often served in pure form: they make rum-based cocktails. The most famous cocktail is rum punch (dark rum, orange juice, fresh limejuice).

- BEER. The local beer is Banks and 10 Saints. Also, beer is sold on Barbados from neighboring Caribbean islands: Antiguan Wadadli, Dominican Kubuli, Jamaican Red Stripe, Trinidad Carib and other brands.

- Be sure to try the TEA!

INFORMATION

- On Barbados, running faucet water is very tasty. It is 100% safe.

- There are often kitchens in hotel rooms (with dishes and appliances). You can save your money if you buy food in supermarkets and cook your food.

- You will not find McDonald's on Barbados, but there are several KFC restaurants. Chefette fast food restaurants are very popular. They offer excellent burgers and delicious ice cream with raisins and rum.

- Almost all products in Barbados supermarkets are from the USA (from Thailand and Indonesia). The selection of products is great!

- Coconuts in Barbados are rarely sold. Sometimes street vendors sell them after making a hole in the fruit. 1 coconut costs 1 USD.

Shopping

Shopping on Barbados is primarily the purchase of local souvenirs. It is best to do so in the shops of the central cities: Bridgetown, Holetown, Oistins and Spiteston.

Shops are open Monday through Friday from 8:00-9:00 to 16:00-17:00, on Saturday from 8:00 to 13:00. Some supermarkets are open daily from 8:00 to 18:00, and on Saturdays until 18:00-20:00.

Fresh fruits and vegetables are sold in markets in Bridgetown.

There is a fish market in Oistins open until 14:00.

It is better to buy rum and other alcohol in supermarkets (more choices and lower prices).

WHAT TO BUY?

- Ceramics of exclusive Caribbean design
- Metal products, fabrics, paintings and decorations
- Rum, one of the business cards of Barbados. The most famous brands on the island are Mount Gay and Malibu (natural coconut rum), the price ranges within USD 4 - 7 per bottle.
- Cigars
- Local spices (sold at any supermarket)

SHOPPING MALLS

- Cave Shepherd Mall (Broad Street, Bridgetown, St. Michael) is open from 8:30 to 17:30 (Sun - 15:00). This is one of the largest stores in the Caribbean. It sells perfumes and cosmetics, beachwear and casual clothes for children, men and women, souvenirs, jewelry and accessories, shoes, electronics. Boutiques here operate on a duty-free system (saving 25 - 45%).

- Pelican Craft Center (Princess Alice Highway Bridgetown, St. Michael) is open from 9:00 to 18:00 (Sun - close). This center is dedicated to local arts and crafts. There are 25 shops, 14 workshops, galleries, a wine bar, a restaurant and a cafe.

- Limegrove Lifestyle Center (Holetown, St. James) is open from 10:00 to 19:00 (Sun - close). The center operates on a duty-free system. There are boutiques here: Burberry, Cartier, HUGO BOSS, Longchamp, Louis Vuitton, M.A.C., Michael Kors and Ralph Lauren. There are many restaurants and bars near the center.

- Holetown Chattel Village (Holetown, St. James) located in the heart of Holtown on the West Coast. It is open from 7:00 to 15:00. This is a whole area of shops in the colonial style which sell national-style clothing, art, souvenirs, gifts and home decor.

- Sheraton Mall (Sargeants Village, Christ Church) is open from 9:00 to 21:00 (Sun - close). There are about 120 stores here, SPA and beauty salons.

- St. Lawrence Gap, Christ Church. There are street vendors and small shops on this street. Here you can buy souvenirs.

EARTHWORKS POTTERY

   #2, Edgehill Heights St. Thomas

Here you will find a huge selection of handmade ceramic dishes. This pottery is perfect for home or restaurant. Each piece is unique as it is made and painted by hand! This is a great gift for friends and your family.

Safety

Barbados is a safe island with a low crime rate. The only place to avoid in the dark in the area southeast of the Fitchild Street Bus Station in Bridgetown, around Nelson Street and Jordan Lane, where the red-light district is located.

DO NOT FORGET ABOUT THE ELEMENTARY RULES:

- Do not leave things unattended.
- Do not leave things in the car.
- Do not display large sums of money in crowded places.
- Do not carry large amounts of money or documents with you. The hotel has a safe.

POPULAR TYPES OF FRAUD

On the street, you can be offered a massage. If you agree, then you will be given a massage for a very long time (after you relax), and later you will owe a large amount of money.

In popular tourist places, locals offer coconut or shells picked from the ground, which can be easily found on the beach. Or aloe vera with the words: "You are sunburned! You need aloe vera!"

Be careful - you may be offered drugs on the street!

Top-25 Budget Travel Tips

BEFORE YOU GO...

1. Avoid the peak season!
2. Search for flights early - buy air tickets in advance
3. Get visa on your own
4. Travel lightly
5. Learn a few words in the local language
6. Always have travel insurance
7. Look for traveling companions

ACCOMMODATION

8. Take overnight sleeper trains / buses
9. Try Couchsurfing
10. Consider Youth Hostels (Book hotels in advance)

FOOD

11. Choose local and seasonal dishes
12. Avoid full set meals and «tourist menu»
13. Prepare your own meals
14. Save money on drinks (take water from hotels)

TRANSPORT

15. Get a city pass
16. Just Walk (if you can)
17. Free parking *(almost everywhere there are supermarkets, where the car can be left for free)*

ACTIVITIES

18. Sign up for free walking tours
19. Visit museums on free admission days
20. Go for free (or ridiculously cheap) music events
21. Picnic at local parks
22. Use the benefits of a Multi-visit-ticket
23. Use discounts for students

OTHER

24. Communicate without roaming
25. Save on souvenirs

Printed in Great Britain
by Amazon